EXPERTISE EXPEDITION

Excursions into New Careers

Expanding your job campaign when your search has taken longer than expected

By

CHAD C BETZ

Author of: "The Second Mouse Gets the Cheese" and "Late Bloomer: It's not too late to succeed!"

Copyright @2025 Chad C Betz

All rights reserved. No part of this publication may be reproduced, distributed, stored, or transmitted in any form or by any means, including photocopying, recording, or other electronic or mechanical methods, without the prior written permission of Tanya Ellis-Asbury, except in the use of brief quotations embodied in critical articles and reviews and certain other noncommercial uses permitted by copyright law and pages where written permission is specifically granted by Chad C Betz.

Printed in the United States of America

ISBN: 979-8-9851438-2-9 [paperback]

ISBN: 979-8-9851438-3-6 [e-book]

Printed in the United States of America

CONTENTS

Protracted Job Campaign	1
Remember, it's not always about you.	3
You Are More Than Your Job!	9
Focus On Your Skills Rather Than Past Jobs	10
Translate Your Skills	14
Network Fatigue	19
Pull the Networking Thread	22
Networking Thread	25
Expanding Your Circle of Influence	33
Research Topic One: Where are the Jobs?	33
Research Topic Two: What are the Trends?	35
Research Topic Three – Job Postings	35
Willingness to Commit	41
What are you willing to do?	43
Getting Your Job	47
Review and Translate Your Skills	47
Overcoming Network Fatigue	48
Expanding Your Circle	48
Commit to Your Plan	48
You Can Get Through This Protracted Search and Get a Job!	49

PROTRACTED JOB CAMPAIGN

If you've been out of work for six months, a year, or even longer, you're not alone. Many people like you have found themselves in an exhausting job campaign, feeling like they'll never find a job. A job campaign can be one of the most disheartening experiences, especially when you've been unemployed for over six months. Everyone experiences ups and downs in life, but not finding a job can feel like there are only downs until you finally reach that one up (getting a job) and stop your search. When you're going through these downs for months or even years, it can be an incredibly demoralizing, aggravating, time-consuming, embarrassing, and isolating experience.

Like you, I've been through it. People told me I was doing all 'the right things', but I was getting no results. I started to think I was the problem, which emotionally resonated with me. Logically, however, it did not sit well with me. I have had recent successes, so why would that change because I was unemployed? Then people told me it's harder for people over fifty to get a job. This feedback wasn't helpful since I can't do anything to change my age. Yes, age and circumstances can impact the search, but I was determined to develop a process to find a job.

Addressing Age Stereotypes

Age stereotypes are something older workers have to deal with, but there are ways to fight those stereotypes:

No Energy – Exercise and maintain a healthy diet to keep your energy levels high.

Set in their ways: Be pragmatic and flexible in these dynamic work environments.

Out of Date – Stay up to date with technology and industry news.

Realizing that my job campaign was not yielding the desired results, I took a step back and evaluated my approach. I reflected on how I came to be unemployed, what I had been doing to find a job, and how I could improve. This self-reflection and change in strategy not only reinvigorated my search but also led to me finding a job. The process I developed is not a one-time fix but a repeatable strategy that can help you reenergize your search and ultimately find a job.

My unemployment started in September of 2020 with a video call from my boss. He would never usually call me via video call—it would usually be a text or voice call on my cell phone—so I knew something was up. The call lasted about an hour and a half. I remember the call as pleasant, with some tough topics, hard decisions, my position being eliminated, etc. My boss treated me fairly, and we left the call on a positive note, but the reality was that we were in the middle of the pandemic, and I was out of a job.

There was a reason my boss eliminated my position. Because of government mandates related to the pandemic, many people in the industry were also losing their jobs, and there was no demand for new employees at any level in that industry. That meant I would have an arduous job campaign. As I searched for a job and networked, I found no leads. I had never encountered that in my career. The lack of leads is what convinced me that it was not age that was the issue and I was not being passed over. There was simply no demand for the positions I was looking for.

Remember, it's not always about you.

Acknowledging that external factors can significantly impact job opportunities can help alleviate self-doubt. However, saying outside factors are the problem and internalizing that fact are two different things. During my unemployment, I would regularly wake up at two or three in the morning from a nightmare and, for the rest of the night, dwell on feeling inadequate and believing that I would never find another job. I would then over-caffeinate myself the next day to have energy and end up feeding my anxiety at not finding a job. This self-doubt and anxiety stayed with me during the day and hurt my job-hunting activities.

> **At my lowest, I was taunted by the "Help Wanted" sign at the entrance of the grocery store whenever I went shopping. I hadn't worked at a store since high school. Would I need to go back? I had anxiety-driven visions of myself in the store uniform, working with cranky customers, and stocking shelves to earn some money.**

> **Anxiety and self-doubt are real feelings that can negatively impact your search.**

I was never able to eliminate anxiety and self-doubt, but I found that focusing on reducing these feelings helped me stay positive. I also found that the reflection, planning, and action steps in the following pages helped build my confidence, reduce my anxiety, and shorten my job campaign.

My reflection on my situation showed that I needed to change my job campaign strategy, rethink the process, and develop new target positions. Switching your strategy when focused on a target for a long time can be difficult. The inertia of your search can put obstacles in your way of changing. These obstacles may include:

- **Tunnel Vision:** The first obstacle to changing a job campaign strategy after a long search is an overly focused search. When looking for a job, you can get tunnel vision and only look for the positions you held before. If those positions are not in demand, you can find yourself spinning your wheels and getting no results.
- **Mindset:** The second obstacle you can encounter is mindset. The longer you are out of work, the more you can start feeling that you do not deserve a job. You can see the rejections and setbacks as a reflection of your abilities. It is essential to control your mindset that you are not the problem. The problem lies in the job market and possibly your search strategy. You deserve a job, and you add value to employers.
- **Inertia:** As you continue to be unemployed, you might find yourself getting used to new routines that do not include having a job. You build routines that occupy your day, like reviewing job postings, going to job search groups, and meeting with other candidates. That routine can start to feel like employment, leading you to lose focus on the goal of getting a job because you unconsciously feel like you have one. You can start getting comfortable with unemployment and set goals to feed your unemployment routines rather than getting a job.

When it comes to your job campaign, the adage 'If you keep doing what you are doing, you will keep getting what you are getting' holds true. The issue with goals focused on unemployment routines like the number of job networking meetings attended or time looking at job postings is that you can miss opportunities to adopt more productive strategies. If you are doing 'all the right things' but are getting no results, it's time to look for some new 'right things'. But be cautious about the advice you seek.

As Napoleon Hill said, *'The number one reason people fail in life is because they listen to their friends, family, and neighbors.'*

The average person may not understand the complexities and stresses of a protracted job campaign. If you seek guidance, it is crucial to speak with individuals who have successfully navigated a long, frustrating job campaign along with coaches who have guided others through similar journeys.

This guide provides some options to consider based on my personal experience with a protracted job campaign. These ideas worked for me and for people I have coached. Each of the ideas can be implemented separately or together. The choice is yours. This is your job campaign, and you deserve to run it however you want to. Consider the ideas provided on the following pages.

I am confident that you will find new opportunities and land a job that will help you regain the self-respect and confidence you may have lost during your campaign.

Reading and learning is a great activity, but if you do not translate your new knowledge into action, you are limiting your gains.

Each chapter of this book ends with a place to record your reflections and the action steps you will take. You will benefit more if you take the time to fill out these sections and develop an action plan. Other chapters have additional places to record your thoughts and plans.

I encourage you to fill out the sections and keep a journal of your job campaign activities. Journaling will help you measure your progress and determine what needs to be changed.

/// PROTRACTED JOB CAMPAIGN

REFLECTION

Question 1: How would you rank the effectiveness of your campaign strategies?

_____
_____
_____
_____

Question 2: How focused is your job search? Do you think it is limiting your prospects?

_____
_____
_____
_____
_____

Question 3: How would you describe your mindset?

_____
_____
_____
_____
_____

ACTION STEPS:

What are you going to do with what you've read in this chapter?

1. _____

2. _____

3. _____

4. _____

YOU ARE MORE THAN YOUR JOB!

If you are following a traditional job campaign, you are probably focused on looking for a specific target job. This strategy has you focused on a single point—that specific job. As discussed earlier, your specific target job may not be available for a variety of reasons, so your focus can be keeping you from getting your next job. Alternatively, you may want to visualize your job campaign target as a dartboard. There is more than the bullseye (that specific job) on a dartboard. There are numbers all around and different layers and colors between the edge and the bullseye. Each of those layers and colors represent opportunities you can pursue. You can miss all these other opportunities if you focus exclusively on the bullseye. It is important to have a target so you can focus your efforts, but it may be time to broaden your search to encompass the whole target rather than just the bullseye.

If you target a job very similar to the one you lost, you may envision returning to where you left off and continuing down the path you are comfortable with. Again, that position may not be available depending on circumstances outside your control. If that position is unavailable, continuing that singular search will be unproductive. When you continue an unproductive search focused on the bullseye, you can miss other opportunities that might be great for you.

Broadening your focus helps change your perspective on the job market and how your skills can be used beyond jobs you've held in the past. This change in perspective can help you see that you have value and are more than the job you lost.

Focus On Your Skills Rather Than Past Jobs

To focus on your skills, you first need to know what those skills are. I'm sure you have an intrinsic understanding of your skills, but you may not understand how broad your skill range is. I did not understand how broad the range of skills I offered prospective employers was until I wrote out all my skills and discussed them with a coach. If you reflect on your skills, I am confident you will find that you offer much more than you currently believe.

> Your job occupies a material portion of your life. Think about how you introduce yourself. Your job role probably has a prominent place in that introduction. When you no longer hold that job, it can feel like a piece of you is ripped out. Focusing on the skills you offer can help fill the hole left by the job loss as new opportunities develop.

Catalog your skills: It is important to write out your skills. Just thinking about them won't allow you to take the next step. Start with your resume, write down your skills, then list out your accomplishments and start to analyze them. What skills did you need to accomplish them? Once you have your initial list, sit down with a coach or a trusted advisor to review and uncover additional skills. You will be surprised by what else you discover. You have accomplished a lot in your career—those accomplishments took skills that you offer to employers.

Translate your skills: How will your skills apply to different jobs? When you listed your skills, there is a good chance you defined them in terms of the position in which you used them. Those skills apply to more than just that job, so it is important to translate those skills into a format that can be used for other jobs.

For example, I had the skill of writing a bank policy for a loan purchase program. That is a specific skill in a particular job. Analyzing it can allow you to translate that skill into general terms that can be used in other jobs. Some translations for this skill include:

- Writing bank policies
- Reviewing bank policies
- Updating policies
- Auditing policies

At this point, you can determine if those skills are current and, if not, create a plan to learn and update them. Now that your skills are identified in terms that transcend your last job, it's time to go to the next step.

Identify new applications: Where else can you use your skills? Finding new applications for your skills takes research. Think about all the professions you worked alongside during your career and identify the commonalities between that profession and your profession.

Coworkers **Government Contacts**
Clients *Vendors and Suppliers*
Different Departments *Nonprofits*
Consultants

Now, list the positions you identified that would require your skills. From those positions, list the professions you would like to pursue. Take the time you need to research the different positions. It is easy to write off a position as uninteresting or believe you are not qualified if you do not thoroughly research it. As you complete your research, you will find you offer skills that can add value to a variety of professions that you may have never considered. You may also find that there are new work environments, such as remote and hybrid, that you may have not experienced.

Focusing on your skills may be unfamiliar to you or make you feel like you are trying to show off. Your skills are not trophy items or show pieces. They are products you sell to consumers through an employee/employer relationship.

> **Example:** I used this exercise several times in my job hunt. The position I lost was with nonperforming residential mortgages. I couldn't find a similar position. I listed my skills and translated them and discovered that one of the positions where I could use my skills was setting up a performing loan purchase program. I pursued and got a contract position to set up a loan purchase program for a bank. The person who hired me left the company, interest rates changed, and other factors caused the assignment to end after 18 months. Nonperforming loan job opportunities didn't improve, and loan purchasing stalled, so I needed to complete the exercise again. I found that understanding policies, overseeing nonperforming loans, and setting up loan purchase programs had skills that translated into something else. I found new applications, which resulted in my current position.

You may have never considered that your skills can add value to an employer in this context, but they can. Once you start reviewing your skills and understanding the value of them, your confidence will grow. As soon as you are comfortable reviewing and discussing your skills, your ability to translate those skills to demonstrate how they apply to other positions will improve, opening new opportunities and giving you the talking points you need for successful interviews.

Identifying your skills, translating them into transferable skills, and applying them to jobs you have never held is a foreign concept for most people. Finding a coach or a trusted advisor to work with can ease this burden. Completing this exercise over time in steps will give you the information, confidence, and talking points you need to get a job you may have never considered before.

List your skills below, and be thorough.

Look at your past jobs, volunteer work, and hobbies.

1. _____
2. _____
3. _____
4. _____
5. _____
6. _____
7. _____
8. _____
9. _____
10. _____
11. _____
12. _____
13. _____
14. _____
15. _____

/// YOU ARE MORE THAN YOUR JOB!

Translate Your Skills

Skill ➡ **Translation** ➡ **Application**

Skill ➡ **Translation** ➡ **Application**

Skill ➡ **Translation** ➡ **Application**

Skill ➡ **Translation** ➡ **Application**

Skill ➡ **Translation** ➡ **Application**

EXPERTISE EXPEDITION

Skill → **Translation** → **Application**

Skill → **Translation** → **Application**

Skill → **Translation** → **Application**

Skill → **Translation** → **Application**

Skill → **Translation** → **Application**

REFLECTION

Question 1: How would you describe your understanding of the availability of the job(s) you are targeting?

_____

_____

_____

_____

Question 2: How has reviewing your skills changed your perspective on your job campaign and mindset?

_____

_____

_____

_____

Question 3: How has translating your skills changed your perspective on your value as a prospective employee?

_____

_____

_____

_____

ACTION STEPS

What are you going to do with what you've read in this chapter?

1. _____
   _____
   _____
   _____

2. _____
   _____
   _____
   _____

3. _____
   _____
   _____
   _____

4. _____
   _____
   _____
   _____

NETWORK FATIGUE

You have probably heard that networking is the best way to get a job. From my experience, that's accurate, but it is not a silver bullet. Effective networking needs to be strategic and involves thoughtful follow-up. There is a fine line between proper follow-up and annoying your networking partner. Networking takes some skill and finesse. The level of follow-up intensity and etiquette are important factors in successful networking and can vary depending on your relationship with your networking partner. You may be more direct with a close friend and be more nuanced with an acquaintance. A key networking strategy for job campaigns is asking for advice, new ideas, and referrals rather than asking for a job directly as this can put your partner in an awkward situation if they don't have anything to offer. On the other hand, everyone has advice and may be able to offer new ideas. If they have a job opening, they will mention it when you ask for advice.

Additional challenges can occur when you have been on a job campaign for six months, a year, or more. Your network can get fatigued. Your networking partners can get frustrated that they have nothing to share and may even start to feel uncomfortable around you. You might even find that you are seen as the person always looking for a job, or people might wonder why you have been out of work for so long. Looking for a job may become part of your personal brand to that segment of your network. People who have not experienced a long job campaign don't know that long-term unemployment can happen to anybody or how difficult it can be. If you continue to go to that segment of your network, it can become less productive over time.

Think of networking like fishing. Overfishing an area reduces the number of fish you can catch in the future.

When I was a kid, the town would stock a local lake with trout. On opening day, people stood shoulder-to-shoulder fishing all day. If you went to the lake a week later, you would be lucky to catch anything. Your network is similar. If you find that your network is not producing or, worse, is getting frustrated with you, they may be getting fatigued, so it is likely time to expand your network.

During my transition, my network was definitely fatigued. Remember that my transition occurred during the pandemic, and my industry was downsizing and under tremendous strain. People in my network were concerned about their jobs, and they were only hearing bad news. They were fatigued even before I started reaching out to them.

I maintained relationships and fed leads to my network, but some members still got tired of hearing from me. Even though I was employed in contract positions, several members of my network considered me unemployed and avoided me. That avoidance does not make them bad people or even bad networking contacts. They didn't know how to respond to my needs, so they avoided me. It was not ideal, but not everyone can handle working with unemployed people because of the circumstances and stresses they are experiencing. Another challenge I faced was networking partners seeing me as the person I was back when I worked with them. This was especially true with my older networking contacts who never worked with me as a leader. They remembered me as the junior person who worked hard.

I needed to expand my network.

Because my network was fatigued and I was unemployed in a challenging economic environment, I needed to go above and beyond to show my network that I was a valuable partner worthy of their recommendations. That may seem unfair, and it is easy to get angry, but anger will not help you get a job. I was angry, too, but I put my anger aside and worked toward my goal of getting a job.

Your reaction to situations is much more important than the situation itself. First, you can control your reaction. More importantly, your reaction has a direct impact on your path forward. Imagine you are interviewing two people. Who are you more likely to hire?

1. A person who comes across as angry and bitter.
2. A person who is forward-thinking and excited about their next opportunity.

Avoid posting about your frustrations online. You may get support from friends and family, but prospective employers may think you have a negative outlook.

Anger can lead to a victim mindset.

Why do things like this always seem to happen to me?
This is so unfair!
Why is everyone against me?

Your networking partners will see your attitude and respond accordingly. People are more likely to help a positive, productive networking partner than an angry and bitter one.

I reinforced my value to my network by working for them. I performed pro-bono consulting for some key contacts and made introductions to others to help them grow and helped others produce more business. This outreach reminded my network of my value and encouraged them to give me the recommendations and introductions I needed to expand my network and get a job.

Pull the Networking Thread

When expanding your network, it helps to remember what networking is and isn't. Networking is not making a sale or getting a job. It is building relationships. Having relationships with people makes it more likely that they will be willing to help you get a job, but networking is not getting the job. The best way to build relationships is to take a genuine interest in the other person.

Take the time to learn about the person and their needs. When you can help them with their goals, they will help you with your goals in time.

> **It is important to remember to give more than you take. A network needs to be cultivated. Feeding your partners with leads and information helps them, demonstrates your value, and will increase the chances of getting people to help you.**

Networking is not a quick fix. It can take time to foster relationships and build trust. That doesn't mean you can't get immediate results from networking. When you are introduced to someone, you can use the person introducing you as social proof. If the person introducing you has confidence in you and the person being introduced has confidence in the introducer, the confidence in you can be transferred to the new person, which will likely jump-start your relationship, allowing you to get faster results. A big networking fear is being embarrassed in front of respected people. A networking partner recommendation gives your new contact confidence that they won't be embarrassed by you.

If you are new to or unpracticed with networking, it can help to do some self-assessment to see if you need to adjust your tactics.

- How are you socially? (Are you overbearing or shy?)
- What will people remember about you?
- Are you a good listener?
- Are you a good conversationalist?

Depending on your answers, you may need to change your tactics and how you approach people.

You may want to consider continuing to network after you land a job. Networking lets you meet more people, gives you opportunities for social interactions, and you'll have a robust network when you need it.

Networking can take time to deliver results. Setting your expectations accordingly can help you build relationships and not get frustrated when networking doesn't fit your expected timeline.

You never know where one contact will lead. One person can lead to another, then another.

When I expand my network, I visualize the process as pulling a thread.

For example, I pulled the thread to get the contract position with the bank I mentioned earlier.

NETWORKING THREAD

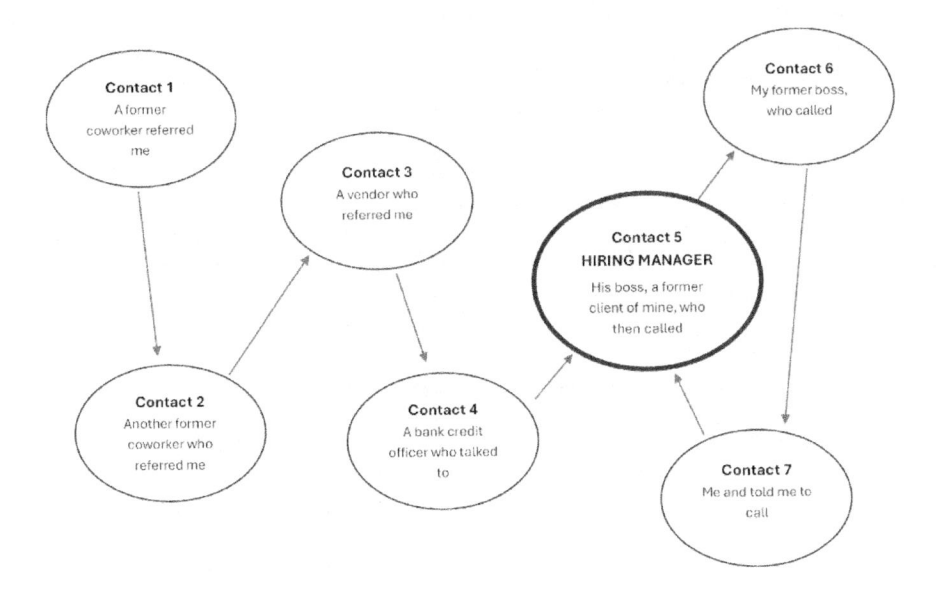

- **Contact 1**: A former coworker referred me
- **Contact 2**: Another former coworker who referred me
- **Contact 3**: A vendor who referred me
- **Contact 4**: A bank credit officer who talked to
- **Contact 5 — HIRING MANAGER**: His boss, a former client of mine, who then called
- **Contact 6**: My former boss, who called
- **Contact 7**: Me and told me to call

If I had stopped pulling the thread at any point, I would not have gotten the job. I needed to keep pulling the thread, building relationships, and making more contacts.

If you are going to start pulling threads, it helps to have a plan. Here is an example you can use to develop your networking plan:

1. Determine where you can get new contacts:

- Asking your current contacts for introductions to people: Targeted requests of specific people you identified.

General requests for people they know in certain positions or with certain experience.
- Industry associations are great places to meet people. Many associations offer discounted or free memberships and event attendance to people in transition. These people know where the jobs are!
- Networking groups and Chambers of Commerce.
- Volunteer organizations.
- College Development Office (even if you graduated decades ago).

2. Once you have identified these resources, develop a plan to reach out:

- Reach out to people you have been introduced to.
- Attend meetings of the various groups and introduce yourself to people.
- Get involved in the groups, take positions, and make sure you are visible.
- Send follow-up articles and other things of value – show your appreciation.

The groups don't have to be industry-related. Parent-Teacher Organizations, Rotary, Kiwanis, Church Groups, and Hobby Groups can be good places to network.

Networking Plan

Person to Meet	Contact to Ask

Type of Network Partner	Contact to Ask

You have the goal of getting a job. With that in mind, while building relationships and growing your network, your focus should be getting noticed by as many people who can help you as possible. A great way to do that is by not just joining but participating in professional organizations, especially locally, where you can meet people in person. To enhance your profile and gain some experience, you may consider getting involved in association leadership because these organizations don't get many volunteers to be officers.. You can step up and show yourself as a leader worth considering for a job.

Groups like this are perfect for getting your feet wet with networking, meeting people, talking to people, and building relationships. The great thing about belonging to this kind of group is that you always have something in common with potential networking partners. You both belong to the group! You automatically have something to talk about, and that's the conversation starter. You don't need to open the conversation with, "I'm looking for a job." You can build rapport and ease into the topic by asking for career advice, industry information, and recommendations on how to proceed.

Groups to join:

1. _____
2. _____
3. _____
4. _____
5. _____
6. _____
7. _____

It is important to remember that not every networking contact will be able to help you directly or even at all. This does not make them bad networking contacts. Again, networking is about building relationships, and that can take time. Also, remember that you need to add value to your network. You will find yourself helping more people than people helping you. A reputation as a helpful networking partner will encourage new people to help you because they can expect help in return.

Not everyone is going to need your services at all times. Through networking, you keep yourself visible to your networking partners so that when you are needed, your partners remember you are on a job campaign and are more likely to refer you.

Consider getting personal business cards with your name, phone number, and email address. I have my photo on mine, but that is optional. Being able to trade business cards at a networking event helps you look more professional.

To reiterate, think of your network expansion as pulling a series of threads. In each meeting you have, ask for an introduction to someone else, whether the person was able to help you or not. Continue to pull that networking thread until you achieve your goal or the thread runs out. Then, find another thread to pull until you reach your goal.

Pull the Thread

When an introduction does not end in the result you want, do you stop?

You may want to ask them to introduce you to someone else.

Like the example on the left, it took eight steps to find the job.

If I did not continue to pull the thread, I would never have found the job.

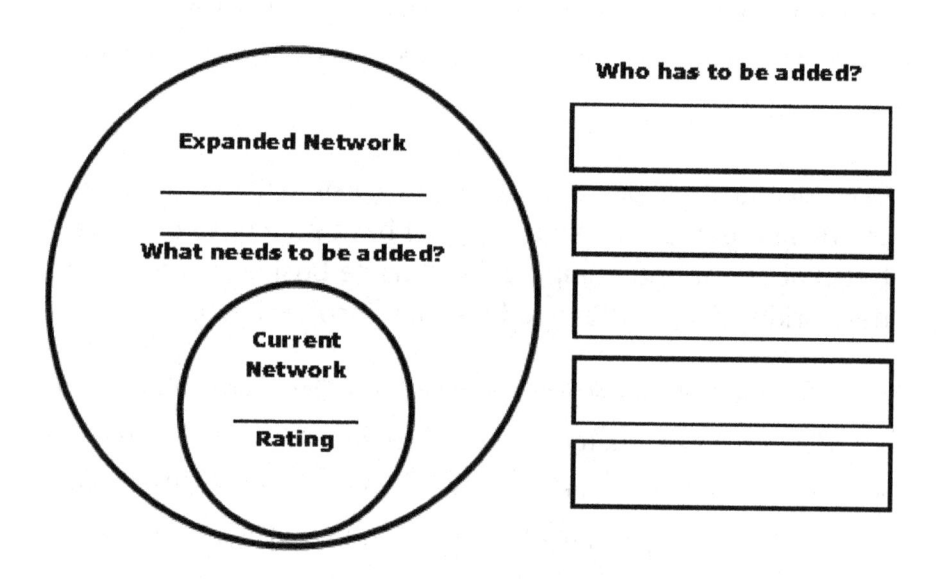

Expanded Network

_____

What needs to be added?

Current Network

_____

Rating

Who has to be added?

☐
☐
☐
☐
☐

How to rate your network

Identify who you need to speak with what industry, discipline, level. Financial Services – Operations – SVP Network Referrals – Introduction Requests

REFLECTION

Question 1: Why did you rank your network at the level you chose?

_____
_____
_____
_____
_____

Question 2: How can you expand your network?

_____
_____
_____
_____
_____

Question 3: List the people in your network who would be willing to make introductions for you.

_____
_____
_____
_____

/// NETWORKING THREAD

ACTION STEPS

What are you going to do with what you've read in this chapter?

1. _____

2. _____

3. _____

4. _____

EXPANDING YOUR CIRCLE OF INFLUENCE

If you are relying on popular job sites and networking alone, you may be missing the job waiting for you. If your job opportunity is outside of your circle of influence, you may never find it. The good news is that you can expand that circle of influence with some easily accessible research to gain access to the hidden job market.

When I talk to job campaigners in my seminars, they ask me if research is "really necessary" and tell me that it seems to be a lot of work and that they don't know where to start. Research can be a lot of work, but it will help you identify opportunities you may not encounter in your daily routines. The research will give you information that most of your competition won't have because they don't know the research sources or are unwilling to do the work. On the question of where to start, here are three topics that will get you on your way to finding your new job.

Research Topic One: Where are the Jobs?

Knowing who is hiring can improve your chances of getting a job. The US federal government produces a lot of free, timely, and thorough data that gives you a good idea of where the jobs are. The US Bureau of Labor Statistics (BLS) is a great place to start: **https://www.bls.gov/**. BLS offers Publications and Data Tools to help you identify new industries to target. You can find out what industries have been hiring and which are projected to hire.

The US Department of Labor is the parent of the BLS. **https://www.dol.gov/general/topic/statistics.** This website has additional information you can use to develop your plan.

You can also see who is laying off people with WARN Tracker: **https://www.warntracker.com/.** This information can guide you on potential industry risks but can also identify job opportunities. If a company is eliminating certain job functions, it may mean they need other functions that you can fill. Layoffs can also be a red flag, so additional research is required. If you see patterns of frequent layoffs, you may want to reconsider adding them to your target list.

The importance of research was demonstrated by the dramatic changes that occurred in the job market from my first draft to the final draft. When I was researching for my job campaign, I found that the government was the most active hiring organization. I had never considered working for the government, so I was missing out on many opportunities. My research showed that the government was actively hiring at all levels (Federal, State, and Local Governments). If you think the government does not need your skill set, I would bet you are mistaken. The government hires finance, marketing, and operations people. I have seen postings for programmers, manufacturing experts, banking experts, and other positions you may not think the government needs. If you do not include government jobs in your target list, you may miss out on potential jobs.

Although there are still opportunities through government employment, the federal government has ceased to be a major hiring force and has even started laying people off.

Research Topic Two: What are the Trends?

Knowing what is happening in your target industries can help you not only in job interviews but also in finding a new job. You may be thinking that trend analysis is outside your skillset or that it is too technical. The good news is, you can do trend analysis without a lot of technical know-how, and as you get better at it, you can learn data analytics, but we aren't going to talk about that right now.

For our purposes, trend analysis involves tracking news and other internet mentions of your target topic. Manual tracking can take a lot of time, so I don't recommend it. Instead, I recommend setting up internet alerts that notify you when your topic is mentioned online.

I use Google Alerts **https://www.google.com/alerts** for my trend analysis. They are easy to use and you can set the timing of the alerts. I get my alerts daily. I even have an alert for my name to see when I am mentioned online.

You can read through all your alerts as part of your routine. I find it helpful even when I am not looking for a job. Reading through my alerts gives me situational awareness that helps me make better decisions.

Research Topic Three – Job Postings

Not all jobs make it to the major job posting sites, and the jobs on the major sites get more responses than off-site jobs. Use your trend analysis and employment research to identify target organizations and go directly to their websites to identify positions to apply for.

Taking the time to research what is available will help you expand your circle and identify target positions you may never have seen otherwise. Jobs are everywhere, even when times are tough. Poorly publicized jobs can be hard to find, so your research will give you the advantage you need to find your next job.

/// EXPANDING YOUR CIRCLE OF INFLUENCE

RESEARCH NOTES

INTERNET ALERTS TO SET

1. _____

2. _____

3. _____

4. _____

5. _____

6. _____

7. _____

8. _____

9. _____

10. _____

/// EXPANDING YOUR CIRCLE OF INFLUENCE

REFLECTION

Question 1: How would trend analysis change your job target list?

___

___

___

___

___

Question 2: How can job alerts change your awareness of changes in your industry?

___

___

___

___

___

Question 3: Which industries are you going to add to your job campaign?

___

___

___

___

___

ACTION STEPS

What are you going to do with what you've read in this chapter?

1. _____

2. _____

3. _____

4. _____

WILLINGNESS TO COMMIT

A prolonged job campaign can produce self-doubt and reduced confidence. As discussed, this can lead to tunnel vision and repeating a process that has not produced results. You work harder and harder. Like a tire spinning in the mud, you dig yourself into a deeper and deeper rut. If you are networking with fellow unemployed people, you may find yourself commiserating with them rather than motivating each other and sharing leads. You may also find yourself shunned by other segments of your network.

If you have taken the time to reflect on how you can apply your skills and how you need to expand your network, it's decision time. You need to be honest with yourself.

ARE YOU WILLING TO ACT?

How much are you willing to do?

_____

_____

_____

_____

_____

_____

WILLINGNESS TO COMMIT

Do you want the results enough to do the required work?

_____

_____

_____

_____

_____

_____

Only you can determine what you want to do. This is your job campaign. You own it, and it is your responsibility to execute it.

If you are like me, you hate being told what to do. The ideas provided here have worked for me, and I am confident they can also work for you. They are flexible enough for you to adapt them to your needs.

After realizing that I was spinning my wheels, I looked at my skills every day for a couple of weeks to identify new pathways to employment. I also spent hours talking with people and researching people online to see who I should talk to. I took classes, went to networking events, and got involved.

To reaffirm my value to my network:

- I showcased my skills through volunteer and pro-bono work.
- I gave presentations, wrote articles, and performed consulting work.
- I committed to new tasks to get closer to my goals.
- I became a lifetime learner, using classes to update my skills.

What are you willing to do?

Do you find enough value in any of these ideas to commit to putting them into action? If so, it is time to start, which can be challenging. It helps to have accountability partners.

- You may want to work with fellow job campaigners to hold each other accountable.
- Set goals that you want to accomplish by a certain date.
- Share your goal and timing with your accountability partner and ask them to hold you accountable.

Committing to new strategies to reinvigorate your job campaign will be challenging. From my experience, everyone benefits from a coach and the guidance they provide. People who want to jumpstart their careers significantly use coaches. I have had great success with my coaches.

WHAT ARE YOU WILLING TO DO?

1. _____
2. _____
3. _____
4. _____
5. _____
6. _____
7. _____
8. _____
9. _____
10. _____

REFLECTION

Question 1: How do you feel about making a renewed commitment to your job campaign?

_____
_____
_____
_____
_____

Question 2: How has your renewed commitment impacted your mindset?

_____
_____
_____
_____
_____

Question 3: What obstacles are keeping you from committing totally?

_____
_____
_____
_____
_____

ACTION STEPS

What are you going to do with what you've read in this chapter?

1. _____

2. _____

3. _____

4. _____

GETTING YOUR JOB

When committing to a new plan, it helps to document it. Although it may seem easier to do this work on the fly, an unstructured effort can sabotage your ability to transform your new actions into results. Trust the process and that things will come through. Be positive and communicate. Don't be bashful about new people.

We have covered many concepts. Let's summarize and bring it together so you can develop your plan and transform your job campaign to get a job faster.

Review and Translate Your Skills

1. Reflect on your skills and write them out:

    a. Review your resume.

    b. Analyze your accomplishments.

    c. Work with a coach or trusted advisor.

2. Translate those skills:

    a. Determine how you can use your skills beyond your past jobs.

    b. Document your translated skills & metrics.

3. New applications – Identify new potential jobs

    a. Analyze the positions of the people you worked with in the past (vendors, customers, other departments).

    b. Document the skills you have to meet the job requirements.

    c. Update and add to your skills to fill any gaps.

Overcoming Network Fatigue

1. Analyze your network:

    a. Identify holes in your network.

    b. See if your partners are fatigued.

2. Find new "Fishing Holes":

    a. Ask your network for introductions.

    b. Join industry and volunteer associations.

    c. Get involved and showcase your skills.

Expanding Your Circle

1. Review employment data.
2. Identify industry trends.
3. Search beyond the major job sites.

Commit to Your Plan

1. Determine what you are willing to do.
2. Put a plan in place.
3. Get accountability partners.
4. Get a coach or trusted advisor to guide you.
5. Take time away from the search and stay mentally and physically healthy.

You Can Get Through This Protracted Search and Get a Job!

Experiment with concepts we went over.

1. Learn how your skills can be applied.
2. Expand your network.
3. Grow your circle of influence.
4. Determine your willingness to commit to improving.

Keep the Momentum Going: Apply These Concepts For Ongoing Career Success

If you are feeling overwhelmed by this process, get some guidance. Your purchase of this book gets you a complimentary Q&A session with me. I'll help you navigate any uncertainty and build a clear path to success!

Good Luck with Your Campaign!

/// GETTING YOUR JOB

YOUR PLAN

YOUR PLAN

/// GETTING YOUR JOB

YOUR PLAN

REFLECTION

Question 1: How will your new plan change your job campaign?

_____

_____

_____

_____

Question 2: How has your new plan changed your mindset?

_____

_____

_____

_____

Question 3: How can you experiment with the new ideas you learned in this book?

_____

_____

_____

_____

/// GETTING YOUR JOB

ACTION STEPS

What are you going to do with what you've read in this chapter?

1. _____

2. _____

3. _____

4. _____

If you need more guidance, please don't hesitate to contact me. I look forward to helping you on your Expertise Expedition!

www.CCBAdvisoryLLC.com/coaching

CHAD C. BETZ

Chad is an accomplished executive coach with deep expertise in leadership transitions and performance improvement. With decades of experience managing diverse asset classes and spearheading strategic initiatives, Chad empowers new and transitioning executives to navigate complex challenges, enhance their leadership skills, and achieve sustainable success.

Having held senior leadership roles, Chad has a proven track record in driving business growth, monitoring performance, and implementing risk management strategies. His hands-on experience in building teams, directing operations, and navigating high-pressure environments allows him to relate to the unique challenges faced by senior leaders.

Chad is also a dynamic speaker and published author known for his engaging presentations on resilience, leadership, and strategic planning. His books, *"Late Bloomer: It's Not Too Late to Succeed!"* and *"The Second Mouse Gets The Cheese"*, inspire professionals to redefine success and embrace continuous growth.

Whether you're stepping into a new leadership role or navigating a major career transition, Chad's coaching provides the tools and insights necessary for success. His blend of practical business experience and motivational storytelling makes him an ideal choice for executive coaching, keynote speaking engagements, and leadership development programs.

Chad is a husband and father of two children. He is an avid believer in giving back to the community and is a martial artist, having earned black belts in several styles.

Made in the USA
Columbia, SC
21 April 2025